God
Bless yu
in the Holy Sp.

Elder JSP...

Letting God Do It !

A tourguide through your wilderness

by
Elder R. L. Palmer

authorHOUSE™

1663 LIBERTY DRIVE, SUITE 200
BLOOMINGTON, INDIANA 47403
(800) 839-8640
WWW.AUTHORHOUSE.COM

First published by AuthorHouse 06/07/05

ISBN: 1-4208-5236-1 (sc)

Printed in the United States of America
Bloomington, Indiana

This book is printed on acid-free paper.

All Bible references are taken from the Master Study Bible ,
Cornerstone Bible Publishers-copyright 2001 and The New Strong's
Exhaustive Concordance of the Bible , Nelson Publishers - 1995, 96

Foreword

Bless the Lord God from whom all blessings flow! I would like to say first and foremost that if you are currently going through, coming out, or been there done that, these pages are for you to rest in the fact that God is the ultimate craftsman of trials and the Master-planner of ways of escape! Listen, God is going to be our very present help, and that right early. Our time is not His time, and when we can't go another step, He takes His eternal hourglass, flips it over and begins to work at His pace, according to His timeclock! What, if anything, you will gain from reading this my testimonial is that, despite what is all before your natural eyes to see, there is Someone working behind the visual.

Know this, God is the ultimate Teacher! What you or I ever go through in this life is working together for our good. The lessons we take to our spiritual enrichment, build us up to where we belong, and we're able to decrease so God can increase! Someone said, "No cross, no crown!" How right that is! If we can't allow our flesh to be bruised up a bit, He can't get the victory. Look at your circumstance right now. Now through faith and nothing else but faith, just laugh! No, this is not a new "laughter movement ", but we're laughing at the fact that we won't be worried anymore! "Master we perish! ", ha-ha-ha! How silly is that! The Creator Himself is with us in our shortcomings and we're sick, up all night, pill-addicted, STOP! Just start to giggle, then tomorrow maybe, build up to a chuckle, then by the weeks end start laughing at "How is He going to pull me out this time?".

When we let go, and let God do what it is He does,we are healthier, we are stress-free, we are more productive for His use, and everybody likes being around us. Look, my sister, my brother, some people want you to make it and others just wish you'd get over it. The main thing is since we are "compacted together", we must cohabitate this green rock until the Master returns, so the more positive Christian we can be the better we are to be around. At this very moment, my family and I are going through the hardest trial ever. I'm believing though that God has directed me to "Write the vision and make it plain! ", and so I begin to write. By the time I finish this testimonial, God will have delivered us! We are confident in this fact and you should be as confident as we are for the same God we serve , you serve also! God bless you!

Acknowledgements

I would first acknowledge the Lord Jesus who has brought me this far and by Him I stand! I want to thank my wife Linda , my better half, and my daughter Talisa for blessing us over and over and over.

To my mentor and teacher Bishop Gus Swain Jr. who God directed me to for such a time as this.

Never forgetting my first teacher of the ways of God, my mother Helen, for showing me early that if you think He can, He will!

To all the ministers and elders of the gospel who've prayed and stayed with me through thick and thin, you know who you are!

Table Of Contents

Always the Last To Know

It's here, so deal with it according to the way God says to deal with it and when He shows up you can have gladness and joy in the Holy Ghost!

Lesson in I Peter 4:12

We are a very patterned creation aren't we? We start our day ,hopefully in meditation on His voice , and if one thing goes wrong it sort of throws us off a bit right? Maybe one of the kids is slow today, or the car is acting up again. Whatever **IT** is, it comes at a time when we really just don't NEED THIS RIGHT NOW, you know how it is. That's exactly the setting we're in when a trial comes upon us! We're in health, or doing well financially, the great marriage, and then BAM! Or rather SMOOSH! By the time we realize what's going on we're "**thinking it strange...**" as James writes. We've been in something called a trial, and it started like a month ago! We're going to look at a few details of the beginning of a trial so you no longer have to be....... "**Always the Last To Know**"

The **first level** to look at is the fact that in this life "we will have troubles" as Jesus said. If we (The family of God) want to be with Him in His Kingdom, than we'll go through some things here while we wait. That's a positive jump on the things that just happen to us all, great and small, Black and White, Red and Brown.

1

The **second** level is when He decides it's time to try this vessel with a little fire. We'll be okay because we can say with confidence, "the Lord has delivered me always" as Paul writes to Timothy.

Thirdly, let's say it's a month of continual things and you say "Hey!, I'm in a trial!" Well, God is the one with the infinate wisdom, not us. After a month and things are still going bad, (health, wealth, marriage)relax, breath deeply and start with principle one. (every morning, rise and meditate on just Him and His voice and direction- If you can't hear the Teacher, you can't pass the test , it's that simple.) Now if you continue on and the situation doesn't change, consider that you're in a level 3 trial of your faith.

We'll talk about these 3 trial stages in the next few chapters.

The Creator

The first thing you should know is that I'm not like your average writer. I haven't studied at the finest literary schools, or been tutored by a gifted writor figure. What I lack in writing degrees though, I'm sure I'll make up in enthusiasm. If there's one thing I'm known for, it's for Judah-like praise! The God that I serve has been too good to not lift up a Halleluah! every now and again. Speaking of the Creator, wherever you're reading this, I want you to put this book down right now, look to the sky, and blow the Lord a kiss! He's looking, go ahead! Now don't you just feel GOOD?! The late Brother Michael Casey reeled me into the fold with that one and so I'm passing that on to you today.

I remember that day in September 1989, like it was yesterday. We were getting off work and Casey had been talking about his Jesus all day! Man I just wanted to cash my check, get a beer and get on with the get on, you know?! He wouldn't let up this Friday though and I found myself actually listening to him some. The woman he was aiming all that Bible at was drunk, so I guess I felt bad for him. He was a nice guy really, just too much with the Jesus thang though! On a Friday, you know?! After everybody cleared out of Casey's car and went on their way, it was just him and I left. He said, "Man that girl wasn't listening to this tape or me. Here's the part she missed where Jesus says.." And I finished his sentence for some reason, "You're blessed if you keep to his word...", right? Casey lit up like a lightbulb! "You were listening, you were listening?!" I said "a little." He was so encouraged, I felt like I owed it too his hard work or something. I was raised in church, somewhat, but I didn't know about this Pentecostal fire thing going on. From that moment on there was an interest that took over my thoughts, my actions, etc. I was suddenly consumed with the thought that there was a God up there and He just might be upset with me not speaking to Him for oh, say about 16 years. Casey said something tme at the end of one workday that would change my life forever! I was getting in my car, and he said "Hey young man, I want to tell you this. On the way home I want you to know He's watching over you, and you should just blow Him a big kiss as you're driving down that highway!" I was like yeah right! Okay Casey that is far enough! I pulled off looking at him and laughing as I left the South Philly Southern Depot. I could see him looking at me as I peeped and waved at my rearview mirror. I'm driving down the Schullkill and all of a sudden I realize how BIIIGGG the sky is today! I'm driving, looking, driving, looking until suddenly I have a strong urge to do what Casey said, blow God a kiss! I pull over off the highway with a tear in my eye and realize how awesome God really is! Now fully crying, I blow him kiss after kiss until I realize how crazy I must look to the afternoon traffic, but I don't care now and I blow Him more kisses! This feels soooooo good!

This new experience wasn't received at first by my fiance' the now turned missionary. It took some time because we were fully persuaded that what we were doing was right and we weren't harming anyone. If you have an unsaved partner today, tell them as they go out the door into an uncertain future, "Blow God a kiss to the sky today, He's waiting for it." Pray that the seed of that word goes down as deep as it did for me. God will meet you as you walk toward Him!

The thing I've learned about God is that He has patience, and I mean long patience with His people. Halleluah! Thank God for His patience! "It is He that has made us" and nothing else matters! "We are the sheep of His pasture" and that is enough for me! "The earth is the Lords" and that settles it! Listen when we reverse the magnifying glass we walk around looking at things with, we'll see things the way the Creator sees them! Instead of seeing how small things can be made to look big, look at them with HolyGhost eyes and say that big thing is so SMALL! We are overcomers through Jesus and I'm trying to help somebody through this maze called life! If you can, clap your hands and glorify the Most High God! Now I could write maybe another ten chapters on our Creator God but I just feel that this little personalized description of Him should hold you for awhile.

Things Just Happen

Things will eventually catch up and happen to us, but cheer up because Jesus went through it already so we can go through it with PEACE.   **Lesson in John 16:33**

Doesn't it seem like the followers of God have the most trouble with cars, money and marriage? Well, the unsaved have troubles as well, we just have a better time than them Amen! See to be hopeless AND the enemy of God is a terrible space to be in. This is why the world turns to alcohol, drugs, sex, and self ,to fill the empty void left in the heart when mother or father forsake them. We know it is here when the Lord will take us up! But things happen in this life, is that right?

When you go to start your car and it "acts up" for the first time, don't you kind of just shrug it off, get it repaired, and move on to the next project in life? **THERE** is where we need to stay! It happened, as things do, we dealt with it, and moved on quickly. As time goes on, it keeps happening and we loose that state of mind from the first time experience,and we revert to other feelings and reactions. Most of the time, natural or carnal. "Why this stupid piece of #$@*^ !" (oops, forgive me Lord)

Now we want Him to pardon us for loosing our first state of mind! Let's be real. If we only could maintain the first time experience in all aspects of our life, we'd be maximizing so many areas we probably wouldn't need Him as much. Oh-oh, you think that's why He let's "things just happen" , to see if we stayed or strayed from the spirit of first things!? Of course! So many times we read in the Word of God about "returning to your first love..." as John writes, or Paul saying "why have you turned back so soon from believing..." Jesus says also, "can you not stay with me but an hour?.." Somewhere we lose the passion at the beginning to say "Hey, it's alright, I'm talking with God every hour and I know this is just going to be okay!" Remember that!? Let's get it back! The first love- experience can engulf your entire life and bring back the fire in your love of God, marriage, children, and the right perspective on material things which "perish with the using". Things just happen but it's how we react that He's watching for. Getting swiftly upset because we're so far removed from the way things were is no excuse to act unholy. We've got to keep in the forefront of our minds that in each life a little rain must fall. Now that's not scripture but it's a nice saying isn't it? Well, Jesus says "the sun and rain comes on the just and the unjust." Simply put, things are going to happen and the more ahead of the game we are dictates what kind of daily walk we're experiencing with God. Happy saints are in touch with the Father daily. Miserable, down, picky saints are usually the ones that if you could see into their daily devotions, they've left their first estate of wedded bliss they felt coming out the water of baptism, or the infilling of the Holy Ghost, or maybe the first miracle they'd seen. This is where we must remain!

Because a few things happened, we can't end up losing our kids, our marriages, our pureness before a pure God can we !? NO!, I'll answer for those saints who are still searching for anything they can find wrong with my style or scripture sense. SEE!, that's what happens when you get away from the first love experience, you knit-pick at everything even though the other person is doing all they know to live saved. We can't live there church! Let's go up higher in the Lord! Stay with the first level theory that whatever is going on in my life at this time, it hasn't been over a month yet and things like this happen to everybody and God is watching for my reaction and so is the enemy of my soul! In military terms- "Don't give up your position!", in other words,the enemy doesn't read minds, he probes them and watches for our reaction. Don't give one! If your situation is now over a month, we'll talk about that in the next chapter. Lets observe a realife example of an attitude of sheer gratitude. An attitude that says, "If it had not been for Jesus, where would I be, I'm so glad that the Lord saved me! "Yall, know that song?! Keep singing it! It comes in very handy. Look now at the book of Job, chapter 1, and see his reaction to the enemies actions. We know how the enemy sought God to attack His blessed and upright servant. If you're blessed and everyone knows you're upright (not uptight) here it comes! Just be ready. Job is very wealthy and calls on God always (verse 5) He has children that he anoints and asks God to bless in case they've sinned. Do we do this practice? We should. Job, like us, is about to be "the last to know", like we said in Chapter 1. Now by verse 13 every day has been like the last. Just blessings and family events and dinners and suddenly verse 14 is upon you! Someone comes and tells you "Excuse me Mrs. Upright, the Security guard just said your car was broken into." **Slow Down!** Things happen, remember? Easy does it! You're driving home in your CD-less Camry, and as you approach your block you smell smoke and put the AC on to not smell it as much. As you get closer to your address, you see the flashing lights,cops, and fire-rescue and realize this is a bad day gone worse! You're notified that your home, refuge, shelter,has been destroyed! These are just examples of what we can go through on a daily basis.

Now we know the story of Job was written for our learning, comfort and patience, and we hope not to go through all this in one day, but we see it could happen! Are we perfect and upright enough for God to let us go past the "things just happen" everyday misgivings, onto some of the meatier trials and tribulations? You hope so, right? The flesh says NO, but the Spirit says "Bring it on devil"! His strength is made perfect (victorious) in our weakness. Now look back at the day we setup for you. Remember the feeling when you were told about the car being violated? It was bad, but not more than you could bear, right? Wherever that space is that you just agreed on, find it, talk with it, pray in it, get real familiar with it because in this life you're going to call on it again and again. The Spirit bears our infirmities (weak spots). When we get the bad grade from a Teacher (level 1) let's react the same as when we hear a loved one has come down with a mysterious illness. (level 3) We need to be at our spiritual best because the world needs us to be. Yes the world is changing faster everyday, yes the hour is darker than when you first picked up this book, but we are the called, chosen people of The Most High God, and must live above and over our and other peoples circumstances, shout Halleluah!

We've talked about when "things just happen" and how to be mature enough to handle these things. This first level is for babes in Christ, new converts, returning saints, and is not designed for tempering or refining or making over. (On the Potters wheel) These are to show you that all things happen to all people and to look to God in every situation. Later we'll look into when it seems like all that you're doing is amounting to nothing.You look to the hills from whence comes your help and you can hear your prayers echo through the valley of emptiness.

The Created

How does the word created affect you today? Say this right now "I - am - a - created - thing". Now that that's over we can go on to perfection. Why say that, you may ask? The first step to any kind of recovery is to admit you have a problem. Now if you're reading this book and going through a trial of significant length, or a mini-trial, the truth to the whole matter is to "fear God, and keep His comandments". If you think you're doing a wonderful job you still have to be humble. If you sincerely believe in your HolyGhost heart of hearts that this trial is to make you strong and it's not a good ole' spanking, you still need to stay on your face in the presence of a holy God!

Being created means we have no rights except what God allows. We come to God with bags and bags of useless garbage to the kingdom of His dear Son Jesus. Don't root through the garbage of the past looking for anything redemptive , throw it all out and come to Him on bended knee!

Being created means my life is being edited and revised at the same time. Edited, because without Him I don't know what to say or how to say it, and revised because He's making me brand new this very moment! Shout yes! Say glory! He has created us in His image, and we shouldn't want to change that one bit! I'm happy in my spirit today because "while I was in my mothers womb, you knew me"! Do you see the implications of that alone?! While we were just embryo, God blew us a kiss! God sees the greatness in us at this stage when we can't see it and we're right at the brink of it.

A created thing has no emotion unless the Creator puts it in. Here's an example. Say you were entering into a robotic contest. You could make any size or type of robot and it had to be mobile by remote control. What if you called this robot Mankind and entered it into the show. Robots can't give impulsive emotion. They can be programed to show emotion though. If the robot was bumped in the contest, would it say excuse me? Would it laugh at opposing robots in trouble? No, but we're not robots. We should say excuse me, and we should help instead of doing harm but many of us don't. We forget that there's a God that sits high and looks low. We've been given what all His creation wasn't. A free will. That shows how great our God is. To make a world of followers wouldn't have glorified Him as a world of free willed candidates of His mercy did. The created has a choice. Do your thang, do what you want to do , or "Remember thy Creator in the days of thy youth ". Let's chose life rather than death. "To be carnal minded is death" so lets' chose life and peace!

The created thing is in the image of the creator. I don't know if anyone as kids watched the Saturday Afternoon T.V. Movies of a certain adventurer named Sinbad. He had to go to lost islands and find miniature princesses and golden talking owls! There was much for a young child as I was to be enthralled in! Well he had an enemy, a kind of sorceror who could change his clay models into living deadly things! There was a catch to it though! Everytime he brought one of these devilish things to life, he himself grew years older! The created thing had taken something from the creator, and so should we be. When the unsaved are being wild in our midst we should be able to say "Peace, and be still!" When those of unregenerated beliefs try and embarrass us for their amusement, just say "Believe me for my works sake". Now if you've been acting a fool with them this statement might not pull any weight with them, Amen?

The thing to remember is that since we've been regenerated, we have a new mind and heart that now moves to different paths in life. Our newness is of God and should be drawn to godly persons, places, and things. Easier said then done huh?, well actually if we live life without ceilings, we'll have a closer walk with Him as the created!

Looking back to the Garden of first things, remember how life was so simple for the created couple? Grass, fields, animals, fruit, all you could ask for. There also was a test for them as a couple to pass! Man was created to guard the weaker vessel and therefore the punishment started at the top, not the bottom. To this day, man is still suffering for his lack of duty and honor to God toward his wife.

But look at God. He still allowed us to partake of His eternal attributes by coming as Jesus to give the Holy Ghost! God as man had two eyes, but the eyes of the Lord are in every place! God as man had two hands but God eternal has the universe in the span of His hand! God as man had two feet but Heaven is His throne and the earth His footstool! God as man had a broken heart, and here do we see the created with the attributes of the Creator because how many times did the Hebrew children grieve God and brake His heart? So then we are the created and we have little pieces of God in us we just have to find them out by finding Him out in His Word. Here again is the created Word that became flesh, with the attributes of the Creator!

Now that we know who we are, how should we act? We should walk circumspect redeeming the time right? Yeah Lord! What about when your brother or sister is just "going back to Egypt" doing and saying what they're big enough to say to you? Do you: A) Ask is this a round trip to Egypt and punch them out!? B) Take out a cord and whip them in the name....? or C) Ahh C, the inevitable answer C. You know this is the answer right? Anything but the first two right? Well tell me why fights existed in the early church and continue to this day? We're not living as the CREATED! We weren't created for fighting each other but esteeming each other better than our selves! We weren't made to be burning holes in the backs of peoples sanctified heads, but to look on the things of others more than our own! Created people love and get love in return.

Remember in the beginning of this chapter we said "I... am.. ..a...created...thing". Think about what you thought at first, and since you've read that to now. Haven't you evolved some either by laughing or by thought processing? Sure you have, know why? You know your brothers' going to tell you why right? Because God moves and so we move and live and have our being! We change because God does. Not His ways because He's already perfect. We try and catch up to where and what God is doing and because He's not limited by time, it seems

He's changed our situations. Actually, our situations are already seen by God as one step: past, present and end as ONE STEP! By the time we get in the Holy Ghost and catch up, it looks like God has changed our problems and we say "Glory!" and all that don't we?!

What we're doing is getting like our Creator in that we call those things that are not as though they were. This is being timeless, boundariless, ceilingless living, that will take us another step to being as perfect as He is! Then we can say to our problems, **"Problem, I see you as a present thing, but God saw you as a previous thing, and by faith WE see you as an ENDING thing, so be gone!"** Oh shout with me for just a second!

When we say in the Holy Ghost, what does that do for you? Well since I can't hear your response, I'll tell you biblically what it should do for you. Go to **Revelation Chapter 1: 10 and also Chapter 4: 2.** Do you see and feel the deepness that the Spirit can take you to? Well, let's not forget the horrible trial John the Revelator had to endure to get this deep in the Spirit. We as the Created, can get so close to God our Creator on His Spirit side, by going through the same sufferings He endured on His human side.

Just meditate like I'm doing right now on that for a few minutes, okay?.

Okay. Listen, as I started this book, I told you, I'm enduring the trial of my life and I'm yet in it as I'm writing this. With that in mind you have to imagine the leaps and bounds I'm growing in Him! These are definitely growing pains though, as my family is looking to me for an answer to our dilemmna. I write on.

Again, "**in the Holy Ghost**", is not only in a dance on Sunday, it's not a louder prayer so sister so-and-so can hear my "tongues" on the prayer night at your church, it is the solemn, holy, untapped place of your innermost being that can only be found by God! What about David when he danced in the Spirit at the return of the Ark of the Covenant found in **II Samuel Chapter 6?** This was no empty dance. David was not to be crowned King until 30 years old, and Saul chasing him, and the bear, and the lion, and he had just defeated the Philistines, and one of his good men Uzzah had been killed by God for touching the Ark of the Covenant and not being a Levite, whew! Now there's a reason to let loose in a dance! We as the Created must strive after a deeper, meaningful, sometimes painful, walk with Him in order to untap the deep things of God. We don't wish these trials and tribulations on the saints, but look at **I Peter Chapter 4:1-10.** This is a chapter the Lord gave me recently when visiting a new convert in the church. This individual is really going through as a Christian soldier. Their daughter was hit and killed after which their brother has suffered a brain anneurism, and then they themselves came down with a blocked intestine that could've been fatal. I asked the Lord that night for a scripture to give the next morning but as usual He comes through on His time not ours. The next morning I got dressed rather slowly, thinking of verses I'd helped others out with in the past. Nothing. Oh, a few oldies but goodies, but not that **BAM!** scripture you know? Then as I drank some water, ready to leave I sat with the Word one more time and He poured it right in about He did all the suffering first, that we could be privaledged to suffer next. When we partake of God, He then takes part in what we 're dealing with.

As the Created thing, remember we're three parted: body, soul and spirit. Whether you've been born again is not in the equation. Adam was just a body in **Genesis Chapter 2:7** until God breathed into him (spirit of man, not Gods Holy Spirit) and he became a three parted being- body, soul and spirit. The body and soul are one some believe, but **I Thessalonians Chapter 5:23** talks about the three being blameless when Jesus comes. I don't want to make vain disputings, besides, my calling is in exhortation!

So now we know a little more about are Created self ,I hope, and we can move on to another topic I'm sure will lift your spirits. The taking away of the church, or Rapture! Now I don't care if you're a movie star and the only religion you've had is that new wave stuff, what is it called, "Transadental meditation" or something, you're going to get a shiver in your untapped zone in this next chapter. There are some things that us who've been given that extra charge of Holy Ghost juice have to give out or we'll just explode! You know who we are. The ones in the church who can't seem to sit down for a hot second, and we're right back up on our feet again, yeah us! The ones who can't hardly get it out in a testimony service, what the Lord did for us now! The ones who stand out in front of the church when no one else will to try and get that last soul saved! The exhorters, the fireballs, the go-get-em saints! We are the Created who've been alloted some of what He had when He turned those money tables over! Or when He stepped to the plate for the Mary caught in adultery. Or when He preached that first sermon after coming out of the desert being tried and they were going to stone Him He spoke with such fire! We are the ones who can't sit by and let sin take place in our midst because the Holy Ghost now abides in us and if the Creator can't be in the midst of sin then neither can we! We conduct mini-revivals in our neighborhoods and for our churches. We just gravitate to the praise and worship forums. We are on fire for Jesus and whoever can't take it will have to go someplace else.

There is a movement right now to **bring prayer back into the Public School system,** but not without much opposition. The enemy of our souls has that foothold and won't give it up easily. Just as wild as we are about the Lord, there are many soldiers for the other side fighting to erase everything good our God has done. If you take the mind of the Created, it will forget that it was created ,thus defeating the purpose of it's creation. The wisest man on the earth, in Gods words, was Soloman. He said the whole duty of man is to "fear God and keep His commandments" in **Ecclesiastes Chapter 12:13**. These are words to live by even today.The problem is our society in America has gotten so politically correct we're afraid of our own rules and rights that WE set up! A person can put together a lawsuit to fight prayer in a place because it offends their opposing religion and in this country the "right to freedom of religion" means just that! Now we've boxed ourselves into this painted corner, and there's no way out, says who!? **"Remember now thy Creator..."** the chapter starts out in Ecclesiastes, **THY** Creator, the one Creator of the writers of the Constitution and the Bill of Rights! The **one Creator** who they believed in from the English saints where we got the Kings James version from! Not these other gods or creators. Yes, we welcome all to the greatest free country in the world, but we must stay with the first principles we laid down here. This is **America, which means "Gods love".** The one God of Abraham, Issac and Jacob who used these Created vessels in mighty ways and promised if we blessed them, we'd be blessed! If these other "gods" are so powerful, why are their lands barren and cursed? Why do they flock here? Because in their countries religion is forced, not a choice. We the Created for this last hour church must fight to keep God in the forefront or He will "curse them that curse Him".

A Thousand Empty Hills

Sometimes God has us in a place where our cries for help and our much praying are going unheard.

Lesson in Lamentations 3:8

Right now as we speak, there is some serious timber being sent up to Heaven. I'll give a part of my testimony. On April 4th three years ago I came down with an illness while at my job. It took my ability to walk for a few hours and even when my balance returned, I had noises in my ears for months. Wasn't an ear infection. It could have been attributed to the extreme noise levels on the job (Railroad Inspector) but the specialists aren't sure. To this day they're still running tests and checking all the information to find out what, why and how.

My family has been very supportive of me in this trial, and I love them for it. The fact remains though, I'm in a Level 3 trial and there's no doubt about it. I've fasted and prayed and made contact with the Father in the earlier stages, and nothing has broken free yet. This is what I mean by knowing what you're in for. Don't get me wrong, we don't have the total insight on the mind of God or anything. We can though have a good grasp on our lives while we're here, and prepare better for the things that "just happen" , or other levels of trials.

Remember the widow before the unrighteous judge in Luke 18? She continuously bombarded him with her request until finally he says give her her request "Lest she weary me with her continual coming" , and Jesus finishes the parable with "Hear what the unjust judge is saying". The unjust judge grants her request for her diligence, and so shall we be rewarded by God! Sometimes it feels like you're praying just to have something to do in your trial. It may sound like the prayers are echoing off the ceiling and going through the floor, but don't give up! Stay right there because the fact that you're mind, heart, body, soul,and spirit are being poured out lets you know that He hasn't forsaken you. From Level 2 we know we've cleansed ourselves afresh and restarted our walk anew so it's not a sin issue. Relax and trust that the darkest hour is before the dawn, the breaking of day WILL come! Just as the evening and the day passed on the first days of creation, the evening and the day shall pass on your situation. The thousand empty hills will be filled again in your life! Those cattle will start coming to graze again! The lost livestock will be replenished and you will walk amongst the blessed, you'll see! I'm saying this right this moment having not seen a cattle sighting in over two years! , but I know my Redeemer liveth! , and he ever liveth to make intercession for me (Hebrews 7: 25). I'm stating the unseeable as though I see it on a clear day. How? Because for one, experience does work in you some patience and with some patience you can see the trial level you're in clearly enough to not overreact or make any sudden bad moves. When the hills are empty, say Halleuah! I must need some quiet time! Listen, when you're on an operating table, and any sudden move can be fatal, you won't move because they sedate you. Well, ask God to keep you spiritually sedated until you come out! It is in the quiet, emptiness of the storm where we can catch our breath, brace ourselves, and prepare to weather out the rest of the trial period. The worst may be yet coming, or, there may be a breaking of day for you very soon.

Either way, we know where we are, we can't get out, and the Master of the sea is with us. Get some rest tonight with the Master sleeping right beside you in your storm!

When the hills are empty your voice will echo so loud you'll feel that you're all alone. This is what we'll call the Level Two. This trial is to bring you back to "your first love", as found in Revelation chapter 2.

You've tuned God out of your life so much that now you just can't hear what He's saying anymore. It's like the husband who sits at the breakfast table with the newspaper up over his face and tunes out the wife who so desperately needs to talk. "uh-huh, yes dear, uh-huh, your right dear....." Get the picture? If we treat God like this, He feels like the neglected wife/husband and is saying things that we no longer have an ear for. Well, just like the wife, one day across the table will come, "I'm leaving you today!" And what is our response? "Uh-huh, yes dear, uh-huh, yes dear", and in the day of our calamity when we put down our newspaper (flesh) God has left us! We can't hear God and the news at the same time! We can't hear God and the radio at the same time! In order to get off this level, we have to adjust our time schedule and give God at least a tenth of our time! A 10th is all! 24 hours in a day right? 8 to sleep which leaves 16. Now He doesn't require your sleeptime, so we'll start with 16 hours. We average around 8 working hours a day, so we're left with 8 hours. 8 hours is equal to 480 minutes. A 10th of 480 minutes is 48 minutes! A little over a half an hour a day is not much to give to the Lord in meditation or reading or prayer.

This is a start to having an ear to hear what God is trying to tell you. Don't you want to get off this wheel? Don't you want to have the pause button pushed again to restart your life again? The truth is, if we don't learn from our mistakes in the past, we'll repeat them in the future. While in this state of waiting, you must continue in the work of the Lord. Be more careful for the things of others. Remember, Job stayed in his trial until he prayed for his friends and then God let him out of "captivity ". My empty hills suddenly were filled with the echos of Gods voice! It sounded so good! I was on my face again , waiting to hear something, anything, and He said into my mind in golden handwriting, "Let Me Do It!" I jumped up off the floor and danced in my tears saying to my wife, "he's going to move! He's going to do something! "The next morning He sent a brother in a local church to my doorstep to start a cleaning business even in the midst of my worse health and wealth crisis! For yourself, family, or the church, start over. Go back to the beginning and give Him your early morning with some meditation and quiet prayer and reading. He'll begin speaking again because He's faithful. Amen.

There Shall Be Light

I can see the breaking of day! Say that with me again. I can see the breaking of day! Whether you 're reading this book as a critic, or as a person going through right now, that statement declares that God is sovereign! We make mistakes, but there's hope! We stumble at this walk, but because He lives I can face tommorow!

Right now in my life I see some workings that tell me God is moving on my familys' behalf. Through this last year of hardship, though I count it all joy, I've been weakened. Oh, we've been fasting and attending and everything, but the fight has taken a toll on all of us. When you go through you're wilderness bout, siphen the Spirit slowly like a rationing in the military. Don't try and stay "on top" too much, as "the battle is not to the swift" okay?

There shall be light, but before that there shall be darkness! Ever since the events of September 11th, 2001, life has gotten darker. People are genuinely afraid of what they think is the end of the world! Whether the end has come or not we only know that we must continue to get that last Christian saved amen?! I'm not trying to bring you down with my story and my circumstance, but I firmly believe that through this trial, God is going to give someone else renewed strength by delivering us IN the fire!

There has been a war of indecision, versus the faith that in Gods' time He will deliver. Ever felt that!? The enemy will bombard you with thoughts of uncertainty if you let him. **Don't!** Stay prayed up, fasted up, so even if the gates of hell attack they won't prevail!

Earlier I said how God blessed with the cleaning business. Well, He blessed it with miracle money from nowhere! and then , **He did it again!** The same amount! It came pressed down, shook together, and ran over to our house and men gave it into our bosom! Then it happened again! This time in the mail again!

Are you shouting with them that shout!? Rejoice in the God of our salvation from whom ALL blessings flow! Now don't think that as all this is happening, the enemy is licking his wounds. He's planning a counter attack as sure as God is opening up the windows of Heaven.

The reason these attacks seem so timely is because he, like God, resides in the spirit realm, so when that window opens there's a glory that fills Heaven. The enemy can see it and mounts a counter attack against the hand of God in our lives! This is why we must live for the light and not the darkness around us. The past few days there's been a crazed sniper shooting people at random in the Washington, DC area. We must look to Jesus now! These are the perilous times to come that Paul spoke of in **II Timothy 3**. Now for the unsaved as well as some born again believers, this is scary! Some who,ve just come into the faith of Jesus are probably wondering how is God allowing this to happen to innocent people? Just like the deaths after 9/11/01 of the anthrax virus. Just like the crack babies born addicted to drugs and some dying before they've actually lived. Where is this light these people keep teaching and preaching about?! Well to the new convert, I direct you to the book of **Psalms Chapter 94**. Here David cries out for God to show up! The people are being killed for doing no wrong! There seems to be nothing we can do! Sound familiar? Of course, because the enemy is timeless and just repeats the same terror circles again and again. He figures, "No one can live past a generation like me so they won't understand I've already done this before!" The truth is, that's right, but, we have the truth in this Word of God and history is just being played out again. It seems worse each generation, but it's the same. We live in a highly technological environment now and every event is a "late breaking news report!" Imagine if every event of the bloody Crusades was broadcast into our livingrooms! Or the early church lynchings and crusades. This is all a trick of the enemy to take our focus off the true event of our generation, **the Rapture of the Church of Jesus Christ!** Oh, there shall be light in the evening time as **Zechariah Chapter 14** talks about. This chapter talks about the 2nd coming of Christ to reign superior over those who come with armies against Israel. He will defeat them of course. This is considered the 2nd coming because He will actually touch ground again as He walked the Earth before. The Rapture is an appearing because He'll stop in midair and call the church up with Him as found in the book of **I Corinthians Chapter 15: 50 - 55** and found in **Revelations Chapter 19: 5-9**. This is the great event, the light of our generation! We must hold on to the fact that

Jesus said "where I go you shall be also," in **John 14:3**. Earlier I said there was a person shooting people at random in the Washington DC area. I taught a lesson on the body, soul, and spirit of man recently at my church. After class, I asked the congregation if they wanted to fast with the missionaries on Thursday they could join in. We would be consentrating on the sick , the lost, and this sniper. Well, that Thursday morning around 3:19 AM, the Lord said "**It is finished!**" and allowed slumber to overcome the sniper and he was arrested at an Maryland rest stop. Is God awesome or what!? There shall be light in every situation if we do what God says to do! When we fast or consecrate (whatever protocol is at your house of worship) we show the Lord we need Him "more than our necessary food" as in **Job 23:12**. In **Isaiah 58,** God tells us how, when and why to fast. He also says what the response shall be in order to know that it's been received well! Remember in the Old Testament how the High Priest would go into the Temple once a year to pray for the peoples sins of the previous year? This was called the Day of Atonement. Well if the peoples sins were too grievious , God would kill the priest. He had a rope with bells on it so they could pull him out if the bells stopped! Well now Jesus has abolished this practice if you believe He came as the last High Priest to enter into the temple one last time for our sins! The bells don't have to ring anymore! We don't wait a whole year wondering if I'll die before the day of atonement and my sins unremitted. Jesus bought Light on the situation by dying for you and I FOR the remitting of sins! The enemy of all of our souls may not sleep or slumber, but those he finds to do his will HAVE to sleep! That sniper said he was God! That's how brazen the enemy of our souls is today! His time is very short and he knows it. There's signs in the spirit realm that we can't see, but we can feel! Pray for feeling in the spirit! Most of all, in all your various situations, pray that the Light of the world would shine in your evening time trial!

Look Who's Not Talking

Though God never sleeps or slumbers, sometimes He choses not to hear us. Stay pure and continue to beseech the Lord.

Lesson in Daniel 9:19

Remember the story of Job when he lost everything in a day and then he was attacked in his body by the enemy? This is no fairy tale. If you are a serious soul winner for Christ, a God chaser, then you will be attacked too! This fiery trial is to try you and for you to come out as pure gold is it's purpose!

When all was lost and the unnamed wife of this devout man began to question his faith, where was God? He was RIGHT THERE! When his so called friends show up with no wisdom in there hands, where was the Lord? He was RIGHT THERE!

When you achieve a level of maturation in God, and all who are around you know what you stand for, stay humble! Yes Job was one who feared God and hated all evil, but he also was dealing with an issue of pride. This is where God must deal with us because it was pride that lifted up Heavens' Music Director in Isaiah chapter 14 and he was cast down, stripped, and his name changed. Though "He's not speaking right now" we still are obligated to maintain our integrity with God as Job did.

Pride is an evil from Cain to today ,and fueled with the fire of seemingly rejection by God, will utterly destroy us. He hasn't rejected you if you still need His love. He hasn't rejected you if you are repentant. He hasn't rejected you if you're wondering if He's rejected you because if He did , you would be reprobate and wouldn't be concerned.

When God isn't speaking to you it is not a place to stay in, you want to vacate these premises very fast! Where would we be if He hadn't came back and spoke to Adam and Eve? What about the 3 Hebrew boys? Could they have said "We know God is able to save us" if He wasn't speaking to them? No. The assurance, the hope of our calling all rests on the fact that He hears us, we hear him, and if He isn't speaking than we need to be still and know that He is God! How can you do such a thing you might ask? By leaning on the fact that you have your sins ever before you and none behind! David was a man after Gods' own heart because he always confessed his sins. When he was in caves and dunghills running from a mad King Saul, he was assured that God would show up even though you don't read of God speaking to him during this stage of his life. Joseph was sold into Egypt by his brothers for no wrong of his own. He was enslaved, found favor, wrongfully accused of rape, found favor again and rose to prominence. Nowhere is the voice of God heard from by him until it was time to get out! This level of tribulation has cracked many, but brought forth many more! To not hear from the one you truly love is a heart wrenched feeling. To know you've done no harm to them makes it worse. All have sinned though, and come short of the glory of God, so we have to wait it out until He comes again.

A study was done on chronic and prolonged stress. An investigator **(Selye 1956,1973)** systematically exposed animals to extreme cold and surgical operations.He called it the General Adaptation Syndrome. His observation showed that prolonged stress resulting from emotional pressures, fatigue, or physical suffering produces a three stage physiological reaction in the body : The Alarm stage, The Adaptation stage, and last the Exhaustion stage. Stages 1 and 2 are similar to the stages I've discussed earlier in this book. Alarmed but things do just happen!

Adaptation but I need to hear him! Stage three is a dangerous stage to be in. The investigator found that prolonged stressful circumstance will cause the pituitary and adrenal glands to be strained at this rate and will no longer give secretions. Salt levels in the blood are diminished and the kidneys suffer damaging changes. Without relief from this relentless assault of stress, the subject will die , as if exhausted. We must live and not die! Say this with me right now" **I will live and not die!**" again, "**I will live and not die!**"

When the situation hasn't changed and every door is closed to you and you can't hear Him and He isn't hearing you, we must invoke change! The experiment is just that, a test, like the one you're in right now! Reach God through the same love techniques you used to win your husband/

wife. When they said "I'm not speaking to you anymore!" , did the world end that instant or did you immediately think "I know what he/she likes and I'll let them cool off and try it." Now whatever you assumed they like, you did because you've studied them and you know them. Well in this level three storm, you can't buy your way out, you can't talk your way out, you must do what pleases God to reach His heart, and soon you'll be coming out!

What things does God love? A cheerful giver, so give a smile with that offering and give some more! Halleluah! He loves His children, so you love them. He loves a broken and contrite spirit and heart, so break down and cry to God for another chance at loving Him! He is love, so love Him and learn all you can about Him.

Beloved of Christ, if God isn't speaking to you today I invite you to go to the throne of grace at your nearest Christ believing, teaching, preaching church and surrender at the feet of the Lord Jesus Christ. You will never be sorry you did!

The Waterway

There are things and times in our lives that we can't pass over.

Lesson in Ezekiel 47:5

In the midst of a prolonged trial that we've been in we can lose or gain spiritual insight like never before. Gain is when you take the trial as ordained by God and you relax and let Him do it, while loss is when you moan and complain and figure you're better off dead! "He's given me up to be burned!", you say from your couch or bed of affliction.

You couldn't be further from the truth! Today I met with a sister in Christ at a Family Dollar by divine intervention. I was out driving and "a still small voice" said to turn into the store. I listened and turned in. I got my business cards out and did a little shopping too. At the last aisle, I heard a woman saying to her son in the cart, "**God is good, all the time, God is good, all the time...**". The next time she said God is good I said "**..all the time** ". She looked up with a smile from Heaven and said "And no matter how long the trial may be, God is good!" I was floored! We shared our similar testimonies and gave each others church names and addresses and left. She declared to me in no uncertain terms that this was NOT a chance meeting and God is saying to remain humble before Him and He will bring me out!

34

Remember the scripture "**Be careful how you entertain strangers...**" ?

Well this is why. When we get into the spirit we can **see** the angels and **hear** the reassurance God is trying to send us, but when we pitty-party our days away, God can't reach us. Not can't as in "not able to", but can't as in "not being reached". Get it?

Let's look at Ezekiel. The writer says in **Chapter 40:4** the vision of God's house was given to him. The following chapters tell of gates and ordinances to be performed by the host of Israel. In **chapter 47** he is brought to the front of the house which faces the east with waters running south from under the right side of the house. In **chapter 43** he says how Gods glory shines from the east of the house and His voice is the sound of many waters. In **chapter 44** he says that the way of the east gate is closed forever and never to be opened by any man because the Lord has entered into it. He is then told that only the "Prince" enters into it. **Chapter 47:1-12** is the chapter of the waterway. Here Ezekiel is taken to the door of the house and showed waters flowing out eastward from under the right side of the house. The man-like vision guiding him takes a measuring stick and measures a thousand cubits, or feet. (Equivalent to 333 yards) The water is up to his ankle. They go out another thousand and the water is to the knees. Another thousand and it's to the groin. Another thousand and now Ezekiel has stopped because the waters have become an unpassable river for him. He's taken back to the brink of the river for the lesson. The man says that the rivers are for healing everything and everyone that follows where it goes. Everyone that stays still in the mire left behind shall not be healed but left for nothing (salt). Everything you ever need shall come from these waters forever including fruit, meat and your medicine!

Let's now through the eyes of the spirit look at what is going on here. First of all God 's house is a house of glory and praise! We should never lose focus on giving God some real genuine worship when we enter His house. We know that God is omnipresent and that is in every place at the same time without leaving from anywhere. Whew! Scratch your head and let's move on. His voice is like the sound of many waters and His word will not return unto Him void but will accomplish that which He has sent it to do. The waters is what Heaven looks like when God is proclaiming something from His holy sanctuary! You may have wondered if there was an appearance change around Heaven when God speaks over your life, well now you have a visual aid!!! Waters flowing as He speaks your **ankle length problem**, waters flow as He speaks to your **knee and groin size problems.** Then when your problem gets so big that you can't swim through the bills and the notes and the debt and the illness **GOD WILL sweep you up and place you at the beginning of your deliverance to show you something! This has not come to overthrow YOU! This has come to overthrow your issues!** God is the giver of the waters and if he guided you into the problem He's going to carry you out**! Shout Halleluah!**

He goes on to say that if you follow the Lords word (waters) , you shall eat, your food shall not stop coming , and you shall be healthy by trusting in Him! Wherever He says to go during your trial, Go! Whatever He says to do during your trial , Do! No matter how DEEP it seems to get, remember He brought you in, and He can bring you out!

David writes in **Psalms 124** about waters of the enemy trying to flood and overtake us. These are proud waters. In other words, in your trial , words that seem to come from God will try and invade your meditation time , your prayer and supplications, your everyday thoughts. You must remain on your face in the midst of a prolonged trial. Men ought always to pray and not faint. Gates are very important because they lock things in, as well as out. We have a series of gates that must be fortified for the battle ahead of all of us. The eye gate, the mouth gate, the ear gate, and last but not at all least, the **MIND GATE**. Waters can flow through gates though can't they? Of course. When God speaks to us we're not really getting wet with natural fluid, but spiritual. Remember the scripture, "..For the weapons of our warfare are not carnal, but spiritual.."? **(II Corinthians 10:4)** Here we see that when God speaks to us, His waters flow to our minds because we're sitting high in Heavenly places in Christ Jesus right?! Our eye,mouth,and ear gates are consecrated not to see,speak, or hear of ungodly things. What about our MIND GATE? Is it just swinging wildly open and shut, open and shut?!

Here is where the proud waters, or the voice of the enemy of our souls seeks to mimic Gods voice with waters of his own. If we're not careful, we can be following the plan of the enemy instead of the plan and deliverance of our God! The proud waters of the enemy can come under a type of gate, but we still have a standard of God that fights against the flood of the enemy! Keep your MIND GATE prayerfully sealed up as the East gate of God! Only the "Prince" may enter inside here! Jesus is that Prince and we ought to know His voice (waters) and follow not anothers. We are deep into the wilderness of a trial now and here is where you'll begin to gain some new revelations in God, to be used when you come out on the other side !

The Empty Tomb Experience

*We that have the Holy Ghost must die today, to live
eternally tomorrow.*

Lesson in Romans 8:13

To be a truly effective preacher, teacher, Pastor, or any
other leadership role in the body of Christ, it is crucial that
we go through an "empty tomb experience"! **"What is
he talking about ?"** , I heard a hundred people just say!
Bless your heart because I'm going to tell you! This is a
supernatural happening which was brought on first by the
Lord Jesus, and is continued each time a born again believer
is filled with the precious gift of the Holy Ghost! You see
we are born **DEAD!** Up until the gift of God comes inside
of us and speaks whenever the Spirit of God wants to speak,
we are the **WALKING DEAD!** We may dress and smell
nice, but Jesus proclaimed **"You white-washed walls!"** In
other words, the tombs of that time were painted very bright
white, but inside, of course, was **DEAD MANS BONES!**
Same thing. Without the Spirit of God living and walking
and talking in us, we can really do nothing powerful for the
kingdom of His dear Son. We must empty out the tomb of
our dead souls and be quickened in Him !

Now I nor anyone else can teach you into the Holy Ghost
because it is the gift from above.What I will do is coax you

into a nearer and dearer walk with the Lord which in turn leads to the "empty tomb experience".

Jesus woke up on the third day with all power in His hand and with all authority having conquered death and putting it to an open show! Oh Glory that is good news! That was the original empty tomb experience because Jesus was the firstfruits of them that sleep. Remember, the souls waiting on the Rapture up until that time were in the graves. When Jesus gave up the ghost on the cross they thought it was time to come forth but Jesus then sent them back because the series of events leading up to the Rapture hadn't happened yet. Receiving the gift of the Holy Ghost is just that, like receiving a gift. When you receive a gift from someone, do you work really hard to try and take it from them? Do you have to pry it out from their tightly closed hand? Of course not! Well, friend the infilling of the Holy Ghost is exactly the same as that gift. You have to be a receptive person that's all! Let God do it! Let Him go ahead and bless you by giving it too you! You may be in the shower, or church, or maybe driving home. You know how all of a sudden you feel like shuting off the radio and just crying out a Halleluah praise!? Well , you should. See, God is a jealous God, and He saw you yelling in the clubs **"Party over heeeeree!!!"** Oh, not you? How about when your significant other made you so angry and yall' yelled all night!? Oh, not you either? Well how about at the sporting event, or at that crazy non-driver, or that parent that lets their kid do anything? Somewhere in life you allowed something to get inside your heart, the very corner of your emotions, and bring forth some fire! Well we have to serve God the same way! Shut out everything that is natural and can't save you and just give God a good praising! How good He's been despite the rainy days. How blessed you've been, despite the sins you've committed. You do know the wages of sin is death and that's one payday I'm glad I missed! Amen!? When you let go and let God, you're praise is real with tears of sorrow and joy for the risen Saviour! You begin to ask Him for His Spirit to come inside you and live from this day forward instead of from far off. This takes some real commitment of clean living because God can't dwell in unclean temples. Initially, He recieves us into the fold "As we are" but when we want His very essence, we must be serious about giving over the rest of our lives. How many of us have addicted relatives who've ran one over on us a couple of times? Well, you can't run one over on the only wise God!

God is a loving and kind and forgiving God, and there's no but coming. There's only the reality that God says "I will not be mocked!" Some people think that getting baptised is the end of their problems, but remember, Jesus said to Nicodemus "You must be born of water (**baptism**), AND the Spirit (**Holy Ghost**) to enter into Heaven. Makes sense because to live eternally you'll probably be needing something a little more capable than these bodies we have. How can you be sure that what you've done so far in your salvation walk with God ensures that you'll get the new body that Paul talks about in **I Corinthians 15**? Raising your hand in some dark balcony , does that ensure you? Someone sprinkling you on the head with Holy water, is that all!? Getting in a tub of water and being baptised is only "an answer of a clear conscience before God "**I Timothy 3** says. These are obviously the signs of a person that is seeking God for answers to that longing inside. The Holy Ghost fills all that empty space! We must long for him like a lost love! Peter rose up before a great host and said "**Repent** (heart felt sorrow for sin and a turning away from it preceeded by the waved hand like a person under arrest) **AND** be baptised every one of you (born of water) in the name of Jesus Christ (seal of authority) for the remission of your sins, **AND** ye shall receive the gift of the Holy Ghost. It is a following after Him that will cause you to just be flooded with His Spirit! The whole concept of this book is to show that yes we have problems. Yes we must conquer hatred while people blow up buildings. The way to live victoriously without bitterness is by His Spirit. Gotta have it! Say it! **Gotta have it**! Amen, and amen. Listen, I hope through these pages someones' been delivered or set free from trying to outhink a trial or a thing that came on you suddenly.

We can react to things in life with an "**empty tomb**" attitude that says "**I've been set free from the bondage of this life and I'm waiting on my eternal home!**" In an earlier chapter, I gave some testimony and stated that while writing this book, God will deliver my family! Well, along the way God has done some miraculous things! He placed a friend in my presence. This person is also going through his wilderness experience and we are encouraging each other in it. We've rebirthed a business that he started some 15, 16 years ago. God has touched people to give into our hands the vehicles, the machines, and the contracts to be succesful! Remember when God said, "Pressed down, shaken together and running over, shall men give into your bosom", well that's whats happening. Also we pray for the other persons blessings and not our own and God has showered financial favor like never before, try it! Pray for others blessings and not your own and watch God! Listen, trouble comes and goes. Trials stay a little longer, but Jesus never leaves us. Pray this prayer of faith :

Lord God above, I come to you today needing my dead tomb of a body emptied and filled with your presence. I want to be caught up with the church when you return. I will dedicate my life from this day on to bringing others into your family. Thank you in advance Lord Jesus, Amen!

Brighter than the Noonday Sun

How bright is that!? I got a revelation of this fact years ago in a weekly revival service called "The Power of His Resurrection Week" which was started by my Bishop, Gus Swain Jr. At that time I was under another pastor and us young start-up preachers would all sit together and just have a good HolyGhost time! Well, I'll never forget this one service night when they called for testimonials and I had my new revelation, and I was going to certainly share! I stood up. We were still moving to the last persons song and testimony, you know. When the Worship Leader told me to go ahead, I said my usual **"Praise the Lord ,I said PRAISE the LORD! and let's give Him a hand praise! Oh halleluah!** Yall know how we do. I was about to say "Yall know how you have to pull the visor down on your car when the wintertime sun is too bright? Well Paul saw a sun which was brighter than that. A sun brighter than the sun at noontime! How bright IS that!, I was going to say! By the time I said about the pulling the blinder down, Bishop Swain stands up and says "Okay you young brothers over there, we want testimonies, stop preaching!" It brought the house down as He always does! I was laughing too, but he had admonished me in public and I had never had that done before. Little did I know that some 10 years later, I'd be serving under his pastorship. I needed that as well as Paul needed what he got. A good ole' throw you off your horse WAKE UP Call! I tell you could you imagine Pauls feelings at that moment? Here he is on the way to the high priest for persecution letters against the disciples of Jesus. He would take them to Jerusalem from Damascus if he found any. He's going along thinking he's right in his ways when suddenly a light shines overhead so bright his horse bucks up in the air and throws him. This is in **Acts chapter 9**. You know what, these animals know something don't they!? Remember Baalim's donkey? Remember the lions in Daniels den? Yeah they thought it was their den didn't they?! God is omnipotent, meaning all the powers that be, are from God! ALL the powers that be, say that, **ALL the powers that be are of God**! That means no matter how big your man tries to make himself to be, God outshines him and all the power he seems to have over you, God gave the man headship over the wife!

Don't think God won't throw him off his highhorse if he abuses that headship either. He will! Gods got your back. You bosses that aren't truly saved and reading this, you better put this book down and go repent somewhere for about a half hour, we'll wait.....................................

Okay, now where were we? Oh,yeah the bosses are back and saved and repented and won't abuse that authority against the people anymore right!? Look, Paul did it in ignorance, but the people who persecute you today do it in FULL knowledge! Listen to this passage;

"That they all might be damned who believed not the truth, but had pleasure in unrighteousness." **II Thessalonians**

2 : 12 The people are happy that they're not going to Heaven! Can you feel that!? Happy!

But a few verses above that God will destroy all of them including the enemy with the **BRIGHTNESS of His coming! How bright is that!?**

When the bills are overdue and the cars acting up and you've sought the Lord early everyday for an answer, have hope! **God is so brilliantly bright, He could burn up your bills by blushing, if you'd praise Him!** God could incinerate your car, or the problem in it if you'd worship Him, halleluah! Listen, the vehicle that God provided to operate the cleaning business is an old something! But you know what, we've been to New York, Maryland, Baltimore, Delaware, Philadelphia and New Jersey doing jobs with this van. Just recently though it started to shimmy and shake in the rear. A friend told me the rear axles go on these Dodge work vans. I said Lord, you provided this vehicle as a means to perform the job you also provided, what now?" A few days later, a brother named John told me he had a friend that was going to just **GIVE** away a van! See how it all works!? Our extremity is Gods specialty! When we can't seem to look at our problems straight in the face cause they seem so big , God comes and shines right in the face of them and says "I am God, and beside me there is no other God!" **Isaiah 44:6** That van is running with only 5 out of the 6 sparkplugs giving compression! I saved a workorder done on the van to prove it to anybody who says God can't this and that! Oh yes He can! **When He shows up, He's brighter than our problems.**

Gods favor outshines the dark power of our enemy everytime!

The other day my wife and I were watching **Prophetess W. Bynam** on the television. She was saying such profound things I called a minister I know and said "Man, are you watching "Neeta", and he said "If you don't hang up the phone when "Neeta's" on", and we hung up. We laughed later at a prison basketball intervention we both are counselors at. The woman had me on the floor face down in tears! She , by the Lord Jesus Christ, was touching me to the innermost courts of my soul! The areas of seeding for the kingdom sake she touched on was just what I needed! Yes, God has done miracles with the cleaning business! Yes, God has emptied a few hospital rooms for our fasting and praying! This though was different! She said "If you're looking for the return on your tithes, that's okay, but if you want **immeasurable blessings**, start asking God to use you as a vehicle of seeding! I immediately remembered how a few years back, while still working for my job in the Inspectors Dept. , I met a Bishop named Brown. He had tremendous favor over drug corners in West Philadelphia! They prayed so hard one night, the drug dealers returned to the corner to put up a fight, and all 4 corner lights went OUT!

Here's God saying" I AM the Light, and if you want darkness I can give you over to TOTAL darkness!" Then the lights came back on and the dealers were gone! He also had favor with God with vehicles. He gave me a nice car once and immediately God said "**This is not yours**." A few weeks later at a revival service a famous mother got up after the Word and said "Mothers getting old and is in need of a car and I KNOW God is able!" The Lord told me **THAT is whos' car that is**! I jumped up, went outside and warmed it up for her. When she came out I held her by the arm and said "Mother look what the Lord has done!" She was soo delighted!

This is the vehicle of seeding that the Prophetess spoke of and I'll tell you, when He uses you for it , it feels great! Well, after the broadcast I asked God for some specifics. Debt free, giving our car to someone, giving my work van to a church, and fixing up our rental home thats leaking. Well, in the space of 5 days, God has fixed that house by telling me where the leak was after years! He has spoken about a check coming that will pay off our car to be given to a couple. Sent a check for a new work van and insurance! He even said He'll give me the plans for a community center He wants to open up! Today when I got home there was a check for 750.00!! God is blessing us in the midst of the heat of our furnace because He outshines the fire! Remember. This is SEED money! God will carry you in the midst of your storm because He moves the clouds with the brightness of His coming**! God is brighter than any condition on this Earth ,** am I right about it!? Oh yeah! It's not about the money, but He knows my desire to provide for my family all that was lost, so He's making up the balance for us, isn't that like Him!?

Well you know who had to try and darken the light of our Gods glory! Yes, the enemy is back. Know this, God will shine, and the enemy will work to darken. That's what they do. Tiger Woods swings the clubs, the Williams sisters swing the rackets, and God fights with the enemy, it just **IS!** My partner was stopped for a license violation while driving behind the church van I was taking back to our parking lot. I won't divulge , but the enemy has this round. Remember though, each round goes higher and higher and soon it will be too bright for our foe to stand, and we will win! **Praise God!**

My partner was arrested that day and charged with not paying some fines from years ago. The judge later found tht he had indeed paid those fines. I went to see him while he was in there and he was like a different person! Not that he wasn't saved before this, but he had a glow on him and he said through the phone, "Man, I am now at the lowest point, and if this is where He wants me than so be it! I have a new attitude about God, my family, EVERYTHING!" I just looked at him and said that this IS the will of God than. Some might look at being in jail as a loss to the enemy. Some might say, "those are the saddest brothers in the history of salvation!", (I heard that.) Whatever your take on this testimonial book, know this, **NO WEAPON!** Okay**, NO WEAPON formed against you shall prosper!** It will be formed though. In the invisible, the enemy has the right to invent, plan, scheme, plot against us , and even take his plan before God for final corrections! It shall come to nothing!, if you're IN Christ Jesus. He shall outshine the darkest hour of your trial, and destroy the enemy with the brightness of His coming! Remember and quote these scriptures daily. You WILL need them, Amen. Isaiah 54:17 II Thessalonians 2:7,8

The Gift that Keeps Giving

*The gift of the Holy Ghost is a power packed present
that keeps opening and opening itself!*

Lesson in Acts 1:8

We have Heavens best in earthen vessels, Amen?! We have the anointing of God, in houses of clay, Halleluah?! We have the shekinah of the Lord burning inside these oil holders we call the body, and if Gods power has ever been used through you, shout **Praise God!**

Oh, God did a tremendous thing when He decided that the frailties of mankind needed a little boost. I believe , as many do, that God knew we needed the Holy Ghost back in the Garden. When He cursed our foreparents for disobedience, He knew they'd go downhill from there. Man went from a lifespan of say averaging, 600 years, to 70 and 80 by reason of strength. Talk about a market DOWNSLIDE! If you owned a business that went from shares worth 600 per share , and in one day they were now worth only 70 to 80 dollars per share, **WHEW**!, you can hear people jumping out windows from heart failure. (We don't get THAT caught up in the stocks though right? RIGHT!) Well , God put a flaming sword in the way of the tree of life because He'll be using that tree later in Revelation time, the Kingdom dispensation. If Adam or Eve had eaten from the Tree of Life (**Genesis 3:24**) in their

51

sinful state, they would be eternally in sin, for the Tree of Life is (**Ezekiel 47: 12 / Revel. 22:2**) to be eaten by those who shall LIVE forever (**Gen. 3:22**) not die forever, see how God was looking out?! Look at how God saw our need for something closer to Him, something like.......His Spirit! All the patriarchs had Gods Spirit moving ON them, but not IN them! (**II Peter 1:21**) This was okay, but again look at the numbers: Millions left Egypt in the great Exodus, but how many to the Promised Land? 12 spies sent to spy out the Promised Land, how many were anointed - 2. Gideons great battle with the thousands of Midianites (**Judges 7:1-7**) where God showed his 32,000 men had only 300 that were anointed! God takes the anointing, and uses it immeasurably to accomplish HIS will.

This is why we don't serve God for quantity churches, but good quality churches! Is that good to your soul?! The making of a quality church, is quality according to the scriptures of God, not man.

Quality in Spirit makes for quality in the pews. The same spirit that made the Hebrew boys of a quality to "**Just Say No!**", is the quality of spirit that we need in our churches today. **Power after the Holy Ghost is come**.

Sounds like **lights** after the Electrician leaves. Sounds like **food** after the fast. It is the gift that keeps on giving as we go! If we are truly empowered by the Spirit, we can speak to our negatives, and make them positive. We can love the unloved in the world because love is of God and we shouldn't run out of it until God RUNS OUT OF IT,

Amen?! The problem is, we don't ask for more love each day. It can't continue to be powerful if you don't try it out. Receive power. Maybe for you He gave the power of helps, but you just want to speak in tongues, and pronounce over demons, and put oil on people,etc. The thing is, GOD led captivity captive and gave gifts unto men, not US! So here it is. After the Holy Ghost has come upon you, what have you done with it?! Do you seek to serve with it, or BE served? Do you give unto those less fortunate, or wonder why you can't get more? When we seed our time, abilities and money, God will bless with something that won't run out. His anointing. His Spirit, and with it comes His blessings and His favor!

A few days ago I received a call from my Pastor to meet him at a local hospital. He told me that a Pastor was there who'd been in an accident and lost one of his legs. I'm searching the scriptures for similar things in the Bible, I'm praying for verses to encourage, you know? When we get there, I'm wondering how down this Pastor might be. We come to the room and go in. He and my Pastor exchange names and greetings and we prepare to give him communion as he requested. He's as upbeat as anyone could be! He's joking a bit and everything! He actually covered the leg up that was missing the bottom portion as if HE had done wrong. It went so pleasantly. He really encouraged my soul that if this man could fight on and stay in the race, I should too! God bless that Pastor of Trenton, NJ, and I hope he doesn't mind that I put his story in here. Only the Holy Ghost could allow the spirit that was upon him that day.

That is the **GIFT** of God, without repentance! My Pastor was really used by the Holy Ghost also in that he realized in going through a prolonged trial you should take your eyes off of yourself, and focus on the sin filled, the sick, and the lost. The work of the church, must go on.

Despite our shortcomings in life, the Holy Ghost allows for positive from all negatives! It allows for against the numbers type **FAITH**! It makes room for more and more testimonies of coming through storms and clouds and fiery trials that make us strong! This is the gift I most certainly want to see spread throughout the world today. If we can make it through anything, then we can get along with the other sisters in the church, If we have the anointing of God , we can surely have enough **POWER** to pay tithes instead of some freewill offering. If God is with us and in us, we can stand up as a minority in battle and say "I have MORE than enough with me! ". **Praise Him!**

The Final Resting Place

"for there is a rest for the people of God."

Hebrews 4:9

One thing I would pray for from this testimonial book, and that is someone, by the Spirit of God, helps themselves to a copy while really going through a level three trial! Remember, it's the one when it seems like God just isn't talking to us anymore! When your boss, or leader doesn't coexist with you, it's a bad feeling. You're trying to be the best you can be and they don't even acknowledge you , let alone speak freely with you. This is where alot of saints jump off the ship because sheep need the calming assurance of a shepherd, and that still small voice. We've discussed a lot on this **wilderness journey**, and of course every journey MUST come to **an expected end**! The search for Canaan by Abraham, the Exodus by the Hebrews, the dispersion of the Jews, and lastly the journey for us, the church, is soon to end! **Expect it!** **Heaven** will be our final resting place!

Gods' expressing to me the need to explain that the things in the first days of creation, were all created for His glory! Through trial and tribulation, we are still His creation! **The first day of creation ,** as in an earlier chapter talks about "Light". One dictionary gives a word called "luciferous", meaning to give off light as a reflection. Remember, it was Lucifer who was created to reflect Gods splendor with his body covered in jewels so that when he moved, the glory of God would shine all about Heaven through the diamond, ruby, jasper, emerald, and so on. He later was expelled from Gods throne for exalting himself in a tyrade of pride! Light, can be beautiful, but also costly! It cost Lucifer his eternal home in glory, now what about you? Will walking or NOT walking cost you the same penalty?!

The second and third days deal with water and seeds. My God my God! We could go forever on that couldn't we? The basic thought though is that God made the world of mostly water controlled by the moon and tide effect. Then He made mankind of 70% water to be controlled by the God effect! The difference is this. The waters OBEY the command of God "**not to flood the Earth again**", and to be governed by the moon and tide. We need to OBEY to being governed by God! Seeds weren't quite dealt with at this time but I'll say this. If you're going through right now, there is NO better time to start seeding righteously while in your dilemna!

The fourth day deals with light again, but with a different light. The first light was awesome in that the glory of God seperated the day from night because the sun and moon weren't created yet.

The fourth day lights were the lights for times and seasons and days and years. This was the light used to restrain Saul and burn in him a new light! **Day five** is where God shows His compassion on us with the animals. They are for food as well as companionship. They are the gift that keeps on giving by way of food, clothing and sometimes protection.God also used them for the first covering of sin in the Garden and later for offering of sacrifice for sin. This is a reminder of none other than Jesus the Christ! Man was made on the **sixth day** and ever since than has been in need of the "latter day rain!". Seek the rain in your life, Seek it especially for others. Lastly, on **the seventh day** of creation, God rested. This is what we look for, the rest of God!

I've always been intrigued by the first days of Creation in that they are so magnificent, yet simple. God decided to have a thought of something while in His timelessness. That something came out of the nothingness of invisibility and became REAL! Time itself had started its first tick! God is awesome, Amen!? Beyond the worship of His angelic forum, He saw a frail type of new being on the first horizon... man! They would have physical attributes similar to His invisible diety. A brain, similar to the Omniscient One. Feet, in similarity to the Omnipresent One. Hands, strong like the Omnipotent One! We were created in His image after His likeness!

After all He created, He rested. God, the tireless, timeless one rested. Was He exhausted like we get? No. Did He run out of ideas? No. Maybe He had a big day the next day so He took off like we sometimes do. No. God saw the need for the people to give Him worship as the already perfected angels do. This day of rest later turned into the day of the Sabbath, or rest. After the Lord of the Sabbath appeared, now its time for all the people of God to enter into His rest,

Now how does all this pertain to going through a trial, you might ask? Your brother is going to tell you. All things are created by God and will give Him praise! The trees lift their branches to Him, the fish open circular mouths of unknown hymns, while the birds never cease singing His praises! This may sound corny but here it comes, the fields ARE alive , with the sound of MUSIC, unto our God! Now that phrase came from the movie "The Sound of Music", but it was a perfect fit. His creation groans, trevails, and prevails in waiting for Him!

How do we today get to a place of rest on the other side of the wilderness! Oh, to get to the other side and REST! We rest from labouring in sin and giving in to Christ. We rest from putting our hands in our trials, and letting God do it! I remember when my mother in the gospel, Evangelist Cynthia Casey, said there was a trial in her life where she thought she'd lose her mind!". I thought to myself, "how could a strong woman as herself come to that kind of place"? My Lord and Saviour!, **I know now!** Earlier in the book, I stated some facts found from a study on human stress. Remember the stage where if left there for an undetermined amount of time, the lab mice died from stress. God, in His infinate wisdom, knows if He leaves us in prolonged stressful situations, we'll either come to Him, or "stress out!" This past three years would've killed someone not relying on God for every step, I know this! I didn't have it at first, or second, or third, but, I GOT IT! **Let God do it ,** is my mantra now! Get your hands off it, and let Him do what He does best, be God. Rest in God.

So much has changed with family, friends, and the business since I first sat down here. I recently lost a great friend and minister of the gospel Jay Spicer, our home is coming up to the Sheriff's sale date. But God is definitely in control. Staying busy with Gods business, will take your focus off your business and allow God to move in the way He loves to move. When you're not looking, **BAM!,** there goes God! What's that old saying," a watched pot never boils"? That pot will eventually boil, but look at the time in your life you used to look at something you KNOW would happen! Have that attitude in God. KNOW He's coming on your behalf, but stay busy for Him. Join an auxilliary in your local church. Seek yourself out. What are you "**called**" to do. **Callings are easy for you to do,** not trying your patience. Callings are without sorrow and hardship and misery. See it more clearly now? Rest in your calling in God.

I can't say there's a clear outlined biblical formula for trouble, trial, and wilderness, but you can know which you're in, and what level. At the beginning of this book, in the foreword, I stated that by the time this book was completed my family would be delivered! Did you run to the back of this testimonial to see what happened, or did you patiently wait it out. The design of this book is to show that **PATIENCE** is essential in a long trial! You must show

God you're willing to go **ALL THE WAY** with Him! Well, the mortgage company is sending out an appraisal person tomorrow to begin selling our home. For all the fasting, face praying, seeking, crying out, confidence over doubting, and dancing over mourning, God is still saying "Let MeDo It!" We're still holding on to His unchanging hand! His promises are **still sure!** What He started out in us, He will establish! God will show up! We came to New Jersey all wide eyed and full of faith (we didn't have any money) Somebody preached "Name it and Claim It!" and we ran over the bridge from Philly **in the name of JESUS!** We laid hands on this home we're **STILL** in after these now 6 and some years, and the people MOVED OUT! That's right, MOVED OUT! God has blessed us to have a vision for the land next to us for a Daycare and Community Center and the land has been offered to us! We're just waiting for the word GO from God! There is no way, you hear me, **NO WAY** I'm believing that after 3 years of holding off the mortgage people, that God is going to turn His back on us now! This final paragraph will be written in I feel, the next 2 months as God does His handywork! **The enemy is closing in and that's when God closes OUT!** Rest in what you **Know** God has said.

Just when you think things may not be moving fast enough, God shows that He's fast, but His time is beyond our rationalization. Remember though, our enemy is as crafty as a serpent, we ought to be as wise. When God comes through and there's a window of time before it comes to pass, the enemy devises a blocking plan to take your mind quickly away from what hope just sprung up in you! We got home the other day and Linda said her car had just stopped working, on a bridge! My work van just had break work done and now there is trouble with the breaks! We had to go somewhere that night and I asked her "Are we going in the van that won't stop, or the car that won't go!?" We laughed for half an hour! We have **JOY UNSPEAKABLE** do you hear me!? The world didn't give it, and the world can't take it away!

Yesterday when we came home we received notice of 60 – 90 days eviction! Out of the blue right!? Wrong! For the last 2 years we've paid **NOTHING** for mortgage due to my illness, 0! That notice could've come at anytime during this trial and you should note that He'll do the same for you as He's no respector of persons! Halleluah! God woke me up this morning and after clearing the cobwebs out of my eyes and mind, told me to meet Him **"at the place"**. Have a "place" to meet God intimately and don't compromise that area or contaminate it with sin. God told me ALL of our debts are paid , and to just listen to Him! The reason for the trial was to know Him like I have not known Him. He made me to then lay prostrate and said you are now ordained by me for ministry in my house, not man, ME! God said to encourage and be encouraged for He is fighting this battle! He then said He would show me how to open up and build the Community Center and Daycare for the neighborhood He's been talking to us about. Be a blessing for others!

Ask God to bless you **to BE a blessing**! Find ways to pour yourself into a work **for HIM**, and He'll do whatever needs to be done for you! Know this also, the fact that God can have a communication with you through the Holy Ghost does not dismiss the fact that only one vision belongs to a house! The things that God is revealing to me are to this family and not over the vision of the pastor of your part of the vineyard, amen? Was there any doubt in reading this testimonial book of faith? Did any little questions of the outcome creep into your mindgate? The only question should be **WHEN** is He going to do what He does! never, "**CAN** He do anything!" Now again, the enemy just doesn't role over and play dead when God moves for us or through us. He immediately mounts a counter attack, and another, and another! Oh, he's a worthy foe and battle tested. This job they're offering me will allow me to keep my calling in God alive and baptize souls and witness, do you think the enemy of our souls wants that for me or you?! Never! If he can , he'll keep labouring to mess the plan of God up, or mess YOU up to miss out! I'm going to wait until my change comes! The other day the church drove to a wedding of our Bishops son in Baltimore, MD. I drove. After the beautiful occasion, late into the night of driving different ones home, we were involved in an accident! A car came from my left blind siding us while we were half way through an intersection. The mans car went **UNDER** the church van , striking the driver door and front tire! He damaged his arm by putting it into the windshield! His car was spewing gasoline and antifreeze everywhere! One spark and the enemy would have taken out 11 Holy Ghost filled, fire baptized witnesses and believers! Despite a few aches, **EVERYBODY** was fine, including the other driver! Oh, you better praise God from whom ALL blessings flow! When I saw the total destruction of the mans car , I slowly looked at the church van and.... **NOTHING**! Nothing was wrong other than a cracked plastic hub cap! Excuse me while I take a few minutes to cry out to God! The area filled in 3 minutes with 2 towtrucks 5 police cars and three ambulances! The next day, while at church, the Bishop found out that they waived the towing, fees, and storage fees and will fix the tire on the van themselves! Let us REST in the fact that we may go through perils, and storms, and dual trials at the same time, but God is with us and more than the world against us, **shout YES!** This is where Adam and Eve were you know, in a place of rest. Waiting in the cool of the day for God to show up again and speak LIFE to them! This is our expected end also. To live a life waiting on the direction of the eternal wise God. Wait on Him my dear brothers and sisters, and He will direct your heart and minds in the midst of your trial! I want to personally thank everyone of you in my church, as well as natural family, that stood with us through the storm! I just found out today I won my disability case and the award is pending! See, God **is** our resting place in the midst of the storm! Now the fight is on to keep our home from the Sheriff sale. This testimonial was not intended to put personal possessions over the much needed area of trusting in God and therefore I 'm not going to say what happened to our home and car and THINGS , but this was written , ordained of God, to let you **KNOW**, that God will do it if you let Him be God. We will continue to battle the enemy until Christ's return, but how we battle is so important today! Rest in knowing that He will, and if He doesn't, He can! Cmon, what do you THINK happened after all this !? You better start shouting wherever you are because our house was in the paper for the Sheriff sale , but today **WE CAME OOOUUTTTT!!!!** God made the mortgage people CHANGE their minds! Somebody even payed all of our fees! God bless you all !!!

I want to leave with you this word of encouragement through a song by **Austin Miles in** Hymns of the Christian Life**, 1936 :**

My Lord Will Come Someday

When dark the night, and burdens press, when steep and rough the way.

This hope overfloods my soul with joy, my Lord will come some day.

I listen for His blessed voice, I seek to watch and pray.

I trust His precious promise true, My Lord will come someday.

At early dawn I watch for Him, I watch for Him at noon.

My heart sings o'er the sweet refrain, My Lord is coming soon.

As evening shadows gather round, and darken all the sky.

I lift my head, I cry with joy, His coming drawith nigh!

Some day, some day, some day, some day,

My Lord will come some day.

Through His wonderous grace, I shall see His face,

My Lord will come some day.

About the Author

Minister Rudolph L. Palmer Jr. is a first time author and serves God as a Director of Outreach/Evangelism at his local church in New Jersey. He lives with his wife, Linda, and daughter, Talisa, in New Jersey. He is currently writing scripts to biblical themes .

Printed in the United States
202081BV00001B/55-72/A

9 781420 852363